# STOP BEING A LAZY LEADER

WRITTEN BY
MONICA GUZMAN

© Monica Guzman. All rights reserved. No part of this publication may be reproduced, distributed, or transmitted in any form or by any means, including photocopying, recording, or other electronic or mechanical methods, without the prior written permission of the author, except in the case of brief quotations embodied in critical reviews and certain other noncommercial uses permitted by copyright law.

ISBN (Print): 978-1-09837-938-4
ISBN (eBook): 978-1-09837-939-1

# CONTENTS

**Introduction** ............................................................................ 1

**Chapter One:**
Tom's Story ............................................................................ 5

**Chapter Two:**
Your Brand ............................................................................ 9

**Chapter Three:**
Working With "Difficult" Employees ..................................81

**Chapter Four:**
Team Meetings ....................................................................87

**Chapter Five:**
Measuring Success ..............................................................93

**Chapter Six:**
How to Keep Yourself Motivated ........................................97

# INTRODUCTION

They all just sit there, staring at you. The awkward silence has now turned into a heavy cloud of unbearable resentment and hostility that has become all too familiar on Monday mornings. Unable to continue, you dismiss the group while mumbling the details for next month's meeting. As you walk down the hall back to your corner office, you wonder, "What's wrong with these people?"

"These people"–as you refer to them–have worked for you for many years. Several stay for the paycheck, some for the convenience, and a few out of the fear of the unknown. They regard you as their manager or the person who tells them what to do and how to do it. Behind closed doors, they describe you as an idiot, an entitled jerk, and a clueless supervisor. The only thing they have never called you is a leader. They know what that looks like and you are not it.

*names are changed to protect confidentiality

This dynamic between employee and supervisor is not exclusive to a certain industry or geographic location. Around the globe, employees are working for managers instead of leaders. They are taking directives from uninspired, lazy, and controlling bosses who are more concerned with their bottom line than the relationships they have with their greatest investors—the men and women working for them.

This book is dedicated to every manager or supervisor who has ever struggled to get their staff to perform at a high level or commit to the company's mission. It is designed for every boss scratching their head trying to figure out why their directives are met with blank stares or fake smiles. It is designed for every aspiring leader who wants the respect and admiration of their team but has no clue how to get it.

Across the world, men and women are accepting positions where they have to supervise people. Unfortunately, they have no idea what that means. They know how to do the work. They know how to make money for the organization. They know how to keep stakeholders happy. What they don't know is how to deal with the folks who work under them. There really is no "school" for this. For the most part, people are thrown into these positions with little to no training on how to engage, inspire, and bring out the best in their employees.

I have a secret to tell you. Are you ready for it? When things go wrong with your team, *you* are probably to blame. When targets don't get met, *you* are probably to blame. *You* may be the reason people call out every other week. *You* may be the reason no one on

*names are changed to protect confidentiality

your team gives a shit about you or the company's bottom line. You may have become what so many companies fear and what many employees regard as their worst nightmare – a lazy leader.

*names are changed to protect confidentiality

# CHAPTER ONE:

# TOM'S STORY

Tom had just finished explaining to his team how to handle a dispute presented by a big client. He laid it all out for them – what to say, how to say it, and what *not* to say. He felt good about it. With a quick nod of the head to signal that the meeting was over, Tom got up and walked out of the 17th floor conference room.

As he walked over to his own corner office, Tom began thinking about the conference call he was about to have with his own boss. His mind wandered as he reviewed projections in his head and carefully crafted how we would ask for an extension for an upcoming project deadline. He didn't notice the fact that his entire team was still in the conference room, shocked and disgruntled by what their boss had just presented.

They sat around the table, some shaking their heads and others staring at the documents in front of them. "Who does this guy think he is?" they asked each other. "This is a horrible approach to

*names are changed to protect confidentiality

take with the client. Why couldn't he ask us for our opinion just this once?" For ten minutes, the team vented their frustrations to one another, describing their manager as everything from "cold hearted" to "egotistical" to "narrow minded."

Although Tom was not in the room at that moment, his reputation for making decisions that benefit only him was evident in that conference room.

Narita, the department's newest member, asked her colleagues if this was Tom's usual way of doing business. They confirmed that this was, indeed, how Tom typically handled things, both with clients and employees. Discouraged, Narita turned back around in her chair and continued to review her document, making the changes her new boss demanded that they make.

Over the years, Tom developed a reputation for being cold and self-absorbed. His team knew that their opinions didn't matter, so they stopped trying to offer suggestions. Some employees eventually left the department (or in some cases, the company) as a result of their boss' authoritarian style of leadership. When a new person joined the team, he/she was given a rundown on their boss along with advice on how to "manage" him.

Tom's reputation was powerful. It led people to know what to expect of him. They could anticipate his reaction to bad news, his approach with new clients, and his overall mood when walking into the office. This persona had taken 17 years to create. It was who he was. It was reflected in everything Tom did and the way in which he did it.

*names are changed to protect confidentiality

It was his personal brand. Every leader has one.

Do you know what your personal brand is?

Do you know what others are saying about you behind closed doors?

Do you even care?

In this book, I will share with you the secrets for building a strong, positive personal brand as a leader. I will walk you through the various areas you need to develop to be an effective supervisor: 1) Presentation, 2) Attitude, 3) Behavior, and 4) Relationships. I will also provide you with a blueprint for building strong teams, measuring success, and keeping yourself motivated. The information I will present to you comes from my experiences, both as an administrator and as an executive coach. I've hired (and fired) many people. I've coached thousands of leaders around the world to build powerful teams, fulfill their company's mission, and make lots of money. These lessons have helped managers become effective leaders with strong teams who exceed expectations every single day.

Ready to do the work? Ready to open your mind? Okay, let's go.

*names are changed to protect confidentiality

# CHAPTER TWO:

# YOUR BRAND

Supervisors. Managers. Team Leaders. Directors. CEOs. Regardless of the fancy title, each of these roles require that you directly (or indirectly) oversee other people's work. In these roles, you are given tremendous power. You are not only a "manager." You are *so many things* – a teacher, motivator, disciplinarian, partner, and judge. You may, at some point, be a shoulder to cry on. You may be the reason someone has to file for unemployment. You may be the reason someone has a good day or a terrible day.

**The *power* that comes with having people report to you is tremendous.**

Have you every stopped to think about the power you have? People are relying on you to shape their experience at work. They

*names are changed to protect confidentiality

are relying on you to lead the way, hold them accountable, and *give them a reason to stay.*

Starting today, I want you to take your role seriously. Commit to it. Be willing to do whatever is necessary to be the kind of leader you would want for yourself. Be willing to work long hours. Be willing to do the dirty work. Sounds like a lot, doesn't it? Before you commit to taking on a leadership role, take a look at the list below. If you can relate to any of these statements, supervising others is probably not for you.

- I don't like people.
- I don't like myself.
- For me, people are guilty until proven innocent.
- I want to focus only on the work itself and not other people.
- I think that my degrees/certifications make me better than everyone else.
- I don't care about being liked at all.
- I want a 9-5 job where I can "disconnect" at 5:01 p.m.
- The rules don't apply to me.
- I am not willing to be flexible.
- I am not open to feedback.
- Changing my mind about a decision I've made makes me weak.

*names are changed to protect confidentiality

Okay, if you *cannot* relate to any of these statements, that means you are a good candidate for being an effective leader! Congratulations! Get ready to work your ass off, engage in a *lot* of self-reflection, and make a difference in the lives of other professionals. If you *can* relate to the above statements, that means that you are either not destined to be a leader or you have a *ton* of work to do before you can get there. Either way, I am here to help you get to where you want to be. Today, you begin your journey. Today, you stop being lazy.

*Do not ever* expect your team to be excellent if you yourself have embraced mediocrity. Your employees will only do that which you are willing to model. So, before you start pointing fingers at your "incompetent, lazy, unmotivated staff," take a hard look at yourself and ask whether you are a leader worth following.

Effective leadership begins with a strong *personal brand*. What do I mean by a "brand?"

Your brand is how others see you.

It is your reputation. Tom's reputation was not that of someone you would regard as a powerful leader. He treated his team with disrespect, and it showed in his speech, his actions, and his attitude. Tom truly doesn't give a shit and he's okay with that.

As a leader, you must ensure that the way you want to be perceived is, in fact, the way others see you. Let's figure out what *your* brand is. Ready? Okay.

*names are changed to protect confidentiality

## Write down five words to describe how you want your employees to see you.

You may have picked words like "professional" or "reliable" or "competent." There are no wrong answers; just pick the words that most closely align with how you want others to speak of you when you're not in the room. Got your five words? Congrats! These words are your personal brand. You can think of this as your own personal, walking billboard. It tells the world who you are and what they should expect from you. Now, the next step is to test out your brand.

## Activity

Ask three people to describe *you* using five words. I suggest that one of those people be an employee, one a supervisor, and one a personal connection. Ask that they be really honest. Now, in order to get the most out of this exercise, you need to be open to what people tell you. Don't judge their answers. Don't ask them to elaborate (yet). Simply accept their answers.

Compare these lists to your own five personal brand words. Do the words match? Are they similar? If yes, you have a strong personal brand! If not, you have some work to do. I remember doing this exercise with a coaching client of mine – a young, successful director in the banking industry. His brand words for himself included "controlled," "polished," and "of sound judgment." Well, let me tell you. The words he got back from his selection of five people were shocking. His former manager described him as

*names are changed to protect confidentiality

"impulsive." A colleague described him as "erratic at times." His wife really gave it to him straight. She simply told him, "You are a good person but I never know who the hell I'm going to get with you." My client was understandably shocked. He thought he had a solid reputation, and he did. It was just not the kind he wanted. We got to work immediately.

The job is not done once you have collected brand words from others. You now have to dig deep to figure out how to make your brand words *come alive*. Consider this: if you are not sure how to embody one of your brand words, think of someone you know (or maybe a public figure) who does embody this quality and *study them*. Watch their interviews. Read their books. Study their speaking style. Do as much research as you can, so that you may borrow what you like and make it your own!

You must live and breathe your personal brand. You must embody these five words *at all times*. These words reflect:

- how you should walk, talk, and dress
- your approach to resolving conflict
- the quality of your work
- your overall attitude
- how you treat your employees, colleagues, and partners
- the quality of your relationships.

*names are changed to protect confidentiality

Get in the habit of asking yourself on a regular basis, "How have I embodied my brand this week as a leader?" Keep in mind that personal branding is an active and ongoing process. Your brand doesn't take breaks and it doesn't change depending on your mood or your personal problems. Even on those challenging days when you just want to scream at someone or you're not feeling your best, you *must* stay in character.

Commit your brand words to memory. Put them where you can see them. Some of my clients put their brand words next to their computer screen to remind them of how they should present themselves during meetings. Other clients put their brand words next to their mirror in the bathroom to set the tone for the day. Allow these words to *live inside you*. After all, they will help dictate how you respond to emails, how you speak to colleagues, how you approach conflict, and how you carry yourself as a leader. Take your brand seriously. This is not a joke.

### Strong personal brands are multifaceted.

Your personal brand as a leader may be broken down into four areas as mentioned earlier: 1) Presentation, 2) Attitude, 3) Behavior, and 4) Relationships. I will discuss each of these areas, as reflected in my Wheel of Excellence model, in the following chapters.

*names are changed to protect confidentiality

## Presentation

*Does your presentation match that of a leader who is confident, self-assured, and empowered?*

Let's take a look at you... all of you. Look in the mirror and examine your physical appearance from top to bottom. Do you look like a leader? Do you look like you give a crap? Lazy leaders (or as I call them "managers") don't care about their presentation. They are under the illusion that they can look however they want as long as they do their job. *Wrong.*

Effective leadership starts with your physical presentation. You, my friend, must present yourself as the whole package and this starts with your physical appearance. Is your hair neatly cut and styled? Do you iron your clothes? How about your nails? Are they clean and well kempt? Do you care for your skin? Ask yourself whether your presentation is in line with what a strong, competent, motivated leader looks like. Not sure what I mean? Think about the supervisors from your past whom you admire most. I can guess that most of these professionals took pride in their appearance and made time to look their best each morning. This is because they knew that a clean and neat presentation helps to create the impression of a competent leader and not a disorganized manager. It sends the message that you value yourself, your ideas, and your work. It makes you prepared for any challenges the day may bring.

If you want to be seen as organized and competent, you may want to think twice before getting on a Zoom call with a wrinkled shirt and your hair up in a messy bun. Begin each virtual meeting

*names are changed to protect confidentiality

with a strong smile, crisp clean clothes, and impeccable hygiene. Invest in a manicure. Brush your hair. Dress appropriately.

Send a message that everything about you reflects excellence and anything less will not be tolerated.

Model the idea that self-care and proper grooming are the building blocks of professional success. Show up this way *each and every day*, no matter how you feel. Let your employees see how great it is to take pride in your personal appearance. This will help promote a culture where employees take pride in themselves and their work. Only the best will be accepted!

Presentation does not only include your physical appearance. It also includes your workspace. If I were to come into your workspace right now, would I have a heart attack? Are there endless piles of paperwork on your desk surrounded by random objects that belong in the trash or in your refrigerator? When people walk into your space or catch a glimpse of it during a video call, they immediately get an impression of what you value (or don't value). They get a sense of whether you are an organized person (or not). They get an impression of *how you feel about yourself and your work*. You want to make sure that your space reflects the space of a leader, of someone in control, at all times. Your office should reflect your self-worth and your expectations. Keep your space neat, clean, and organized at all times to show others that *you mean business*!

If you are a manager, director, or CEO overseeing a whole department, building, or unit, it is also your responsibility to ensure that your area is in good condition. This includes the entry way, the waiting area, common spaces, etc. You may be thinking, "That is

*names are changed to protect confidentiality

not part of my job!" You may also be thinking, "Even if I were willing to take responsibility of these areas, I don't have the time to do so!" Well, my response to that is: *Everything is your job* if you are to be an effective leader.

A focus on presentation includes paying attention not only to *your* appearance but also that of your business. I can remember, years ago, walking into the building of a new client's office and being shocked by the lack of care in the building's upkeep. As soon as I walked in, I noticed how dark the lighting was and how gloomy everything felt. They had some Christmas lights hanging on the wall that were missing light bulbs and I noticed a few pieces of tissue on the floor. Even the clients in the waiting room looked depressed. Remember: Human beings are influenced by their outside environment. When our space looks and feels clean and in order, it makes us feel good about ourselves and what we're doing there.

What feeling do your customers/clients get when they walk onto your floor or into your building?

Is the area clean and neat? How is the lighting? Have you paid attention to the décor? Remember, you represent the building, and the building represents *you*. Take the time to pick up the trash that you see. Invest in a good cleaning crew. Put processes in place to ensure that your team's space looks and feels like *success*. I want every client, employee, and partner you have to walk into your building or department and think, "Wow. They really care around here!"

*names are changed to protect confidentiality

## Attitude

*Does your attitude match that of a leader who is confident, self-assured, and empowered?*

One of my coaching clients–a successful businesswoman in finance–was having a conversation with her direct report, Greg. Greg informed my client that he was actively exploring management positions within the company. My client, believing that Greg might struggle as a leader, asked him what he finds appealing about being in a leadership role. Greg had some difficulty answering the question, eventually mumbling that moving up was simply "a natural next step."

*My guess was that Greg had no idea why he wanted to pursue a position in management, aside from the fact that he simply "thought it made sense."*

Greg did not take the time to explore *why* he wanted to move up or what it even really meant to be a leader. He hadn't searched deep inside of himself to explore his definition of leadership. He hadn't explored his strengths/weaknesses as a potential leader. Greg definitely did not take into account how this new role might impact his mental, emotional, and physical health on a daily basis. This ability to identify, explore, and develop your thinking represents the second target area in the Wheel of Excellence model: Attitude.

*names are changed to protect confidentiality

## Effective leaders embrace a life of intentional self-reflection and self-analysis.

Effective leadership requires a particular type of mindset. If you aspire to be a leader or want to reinvent yourself as one, you must engage in some deep self-reflection. Sit down and ask yourself the following questions:

- ▶ Why do I want to be in a leadership position? What about it seems appealing?

- ▶ How does being a leader make me feel about myself?

- ▶ How does it feel to be in a position of power over others?

- ▶ Do I like people? Do I enjoy being around them?

- ▶ Am I motivated to understand others and find out what motivates them or keeps them feeling valued?

A lazy leader does not engage in self-reflection. A lazy leader doesn't care to ask questions or explore their inner thoughts. They don't question their decisions or try to understand their own behavior. They do not reflect on anything at all. They just go about their day, going through the motions. An effective leader, by contrast, *constantly* and *consistently* digs deep. Are you ready to dig deep and analyze what you do and why you do it? Many of you might find this incredibly draining. "Why does it have to be so complicated?" You might wonder. '*Why do I have to do all this emotional work and analyze myself? Can't I just tell people what to do?*' Well, no.

*names are changed to protect confidentiality

Amazingly effective leaders know the *power* that comes from building a certain mindset – the kind of mindset that makes others want to drop what they're doing and *follow you*.

Let's take a closer look at the type of attitude you need to be an effective leader.

**1. Positive and friendly:** Effective leaders embrace an attitude of positivity. They generally see the bright side of things and are quick to point out the good in people. For them, the glass is always half *full*. Effective leaders believe that people (including their employees) are generally good human beings. They adopt an innocent-until-proven-guilty view of humanity.

Lazy leaders are grumpy and miserable. They bring their personal problems to work. They take things out on people. They are quick to point out what went wrong and find it easy to criticize others. Lazy leaders complain about almost everything. They stay to themselves and try their best to avoid contact with their team members. Lazy leaders adopt a guilty-until-proven-innocent mindset.

In most cases, this negative or what's-the-point? type of attitude is a reflection of that manager's upbringing or adult life experiences. Perhaps they grew up around negative people who complained about everything. Perhaps they grew up in a neighborhood so stricken by crime and poverty that they internalized an attitude of hopelessness and despair. Many things can contribute to a negative attitude later in life. The good news, though, is that this is not a life sentence. I've worked with many professionals who have transformed their attitude to be more positive and hopeful.

*names are changed to protect confidentiality

They recognized, through working with a coach and engaging in self-reflection, that a pessimistic attitude gets in the way of achieving outcomes. They came to understand that a this-will-never-work attitude keeps teams from staying motivated or giving their best. They did the work and over time, changed a negative mindset into a powerful, positive approach to leadership, and life itself.

Decide that you, my effective leader, will embrace a positive attitude no matter what. Decide that with you as their leader, your employees will feel safe and hopeful for the future. They will watch your winning attitude, replicate it with their clients, and then use it to sell your company's brand. It's a win-win! Trust me, you want this kind of energy *everywhere.* You want it to become contagious and spread like wildfire to get people focused on big, amazing goals.

As a leader, it is your job to be the most optimistic person in the room. Don't start a team meeting until your mind is right! Walk into the room (or virtual meeting) as if you have just won five million dollars. Be excited about our team and your industry! That means a big smile, excellent posture, and a focus so intense that it gets each employee motivated to bring your vision to life. Let me be clear. I'm not suggesting that you be unrealistic or naïve. I know that life is not perfect. I know that budgets will be cut and business will be lost. I know that clients might decide to take their business elsewhere or that deadlines might have to be moved up. None of that matters! Having a positive attitude is an *internal* experience. It can exist regardless of outside circumstances. Decide that you as a *leader* will operate from a place of hope and positivity no matter what comes at you. *Expect the same from your team.* Remember:

*names are changed to protect confidentiality

I'm not asking you to be fake or pretend that everything will always be perfect. Rather, I am recommending that you look for the good in every situation, so that you can come from a place of strength instead of destruction. Your team is depending on you to find the good in *them* and the work they do, so work hard to be uplifting even on the most challenging of days.

**2. Solution focused:** Effective leaders find solutions! They see problems as opportunities, not stumbling blocks. When an issue arises, effective leaders remain calm and do what is necessary to either fix the problem or minimize its negative impact. You can detect this solution-focused attitude in a leader's emails when they always present a solution or propose a course of action when facing a problem.

Lazy leaders don't offer solutions. They offer complaints. They see a challenge and don't bother to think beyond what is in front of them. A lazy leader might wait for someone else to solve the problem or even worse, they might make the problem worse by highlighting everything that is wrong or unfair. It's as if they have forgotten that *they* are in charge!

Stop reading for a moment and review the last ten emails you sent to your team. How would you describe your tone or attitude? Do you come across as solution oriented? Are you using words like "we can," "we will be able to," or "let's try to?" Stop telling me what can't be done and tell me what *will* be done! Offer ideas. Think outside the box. Find out what has worked before and get started on a

*names are changed to protect confidentiality

solution. Stop your whining, get off your ass, and act like a leader who gets things done. I promise you, the energy is infectious.

**3. Humility/vulnerability:** Effective leaders embrace an attitude of humility and vulnerability. They know that they are worth just as much as any other employee, regardless of their level of education, position in the company, or pay rate. They readily admit to their mistakes and are quick to apologize when needed. Effective leaders don't hide the fact that they are human. They are strategic, yes, but they understand the power of being relatable.

Lazy leaders wear a mask. They hide their emotions at all times, never admit their wrongs, and behave in ways that reinforce a "me vs. them" dynamic. Lazy leaders don't know how to back down from an argument, even when they know they are wrong or it's in the best interest of the company. They don't know when to be quiet. Tell me, when was the last time you apologized to a direct report, asked an employee to share their expertise, or shared a personal experience with them? Putting yourself "out there" for your staff during appropriate times builds trust and likeability. If you don't care whether anyone likes or trust you, leadership is not for you.

In most cases, it is the lazy leader's ego that gets in the way of building relationships with the team. This fear (and trust me, it's all based on fear) causes some managers to shut down instead of opening up to the very people that need them the most.

How can leaders get better at being vulnerable? This, like anything else I describe in this book, can be developed as a skill.

*names are changed to protect confidentiality

First, you must put yourself at the same level as your employees. Put your fancy degrees, certifications, and awards to the side and understand that your PhD does not make you a leader. Your ability to inspire, motivate, and move people toward greatness makes you a leader! Now, I understand that it might be difficult to do what I am asking, because you worked so damn hard for your degrees and you want the respect that comes with this recognition. However, in your day-to-day experiences with your staff, those degrees won't mean a damn thing.

The next thing you want to do to build vulnerability is put yourself in your employees' shoes. Think back to a time when you were in their position – when you were trying your best to move up, get noticed, and make a decent living. Remember the days when you had a boss and all the anxiety, worry, and frustration that came with reporting to someone who was not perfect. Think back to what that was like. You are now in a position of power, perhaps with only a few people above your pay grade. You enjoy perks that only a few in the company can enjoy. You get paid more than your employees. You enjoy certain liberties afforded to a select few. Your experience at work is *different* than it is for your employees. That's not a bad thing (besides, you've earned it!) but it is imperative that you remember what it was like to be in their shoes.

Keep those memories alive, so that you can remain humble and lead from a place of true understanding and compassion for your direct reports.

To be vulnerable as a leader, you need to get comfortable with "putting yourself out there." This means getting used to the idea

*names are changed to protect confidentiality

that you are not perfect (surprising, right?) and the world is not perfect. There are going to be times when you will need to express fear, anger, anxiety, and sadness in front of your staff. Don't misunderstand me. I am not suggesting that you cry to your employees if you're having troubles in your marriage or tell your staff that you're scared of your own boss (too much information and unprofessional). What I am recommending is that you share your feelings honestly and fully *when doing so will help the team move forward*. Do it when it will help build a relationship. Do it to show others that even when we are feeling scared or frustrated, we can rise up to the occasion and do what needs to be done. *That* is leadership.

Of course, showing vulnerability can be a tricky thing when you are in a position of power and authority. You must be vulnerable at the right time, with the right person, for the right reasons. Here is a case example to illustrate how (appropriate and strategic) vulnerability can help build relationships.

A few years ago, I coached a senior leader on how to improve his communication with his team. My client, whom I will call "Tim," was very professional and knowledgeable in his industry. His employees, however, felt that Tim had a wall up, never showing emotions of any kind. During our sessions, Tim shared his fear that his team might not look up to him if he shared his feelings. I challenged his views and helped him learn how to show vulnerability if the situation warranted it. As it turned out, the company had to lay off 50 people that quarter, including some members of his team. Tim, at this stage in his professional development, was able to show emotion during a meeting where the news was delivered. In

*names are changed to protect confidentiality

his message to his team, Tim was able to verbalize feelings of sadness and disappointment. He explained, "This is a difficult time for the business and for our team. I feel sad for our team and anxious for what may happen next. Although I don't have all the information you may need right now, I promise to make myself available for those that want to talk or process what's happening. We will do what we can together and move forward one day at a time. I'm with you."

See what he did there? Tim showed vulnerability in order to connect with his team. Had he not disclosed his own feelings on the matter, he would have run the risk of appearing cold and disconnected. By showing emotion, you send the message that you are human and capable of feeling what others might be feeling. By remaining positive and hopeful, you show that you are a leader who can lead the way toward a brighter tomorrow.

This is what every team needs from its leader.

**4. Flexibility:** Effective leaders are not stubborn. They don't have a my-way-or-the-highway type of attitude and they certainly don't shy away from changing their minds when necessary. A good leader, you see, is like a good sailor. They steer the ship in a certain direction but adjust the sails often to adapt to the winds and other conditions. If you want to be successful as someone's boss, you must always be ready for the unexpected. Learn to expect and accept change as it comes. Your boss leaves the company. Your best employee quits. The company goes through a merger. Your biggest client decides not to renew its contract. Your way of thinking

*names are changed to protect confidentiality

changes. Anything can (and will) happen, so be prepared with a contingency plan for absolutely everything.

Having a flexible mindset might be difficult for some leaders, particularly those who are new to the role. Many employees step into their leadership role with a narrow-minded view of how to run a department. Believing they should do what got them to this point, new leaders have a tendency to approach situations from a more technical standpoint. They stick to what is correct, *logical, and supported by facts (only)*. They become hyper focused on the details of an event instead of looking at the bigger picture. Now, as a leader, they must expand their approach to include a more flexible, adaptive way of approaching people and ideas. Remember, change is the only constant when it comes to leadership! Stay ready.

**5. Confidence:** Effective leaders are confident in who they are, what they can achieve, and where they're going! They understand that while they may not be perfect, they are certainly worthy of their success. They walk into every situation with their head held high, a smile on their face, and a winning attitude.

Lazy leaders quite often look down on themselves and have a habit of questioning all of their decisions. They are insecure and may not believe that they deserve to be in the position they are in. Lazy leaders also refuse to do the work required to build their self-confidence because it's "not worth it" or "too hard." They don't realize that their self-image has a direct impact on their team members. Would you want to follow a leader who doesn't believe

*names are changed to protect confidentiality

in themself? *No.* You want to follow someone who can confidently say, "Come with me. Let's do amazing things together!"

You may be asking, "How do I build my self-confidence?" Well, this requires a lot of the self-reflection we talked about earlier and a commitment to fight for that person inside you that believes you are excellent. For those who need to do this work, I advise that you look back to where you developed your sense of worth. Many folks develop (or lose) their confidence during childhood, depending on the messages they received from loved ones about self-worth. Some of my clients report that growing up, they never heard a "good job" or "I'm proud of you" from anyone around them. There were no celebrations of success and no encouraging words after a loss or failure. For other individuals, confidence is lost through painful life experiences (divorce, loss of a job, illness, etc.). I had a client who lost her self-confidence after working for someone who micro-managed everything she did. Her boss never had anything good to say about her work and would often gossip about her behind closed doors. The manager went so far as to embarrass her publicly after my client made a small mistake on a report.

Here are some of the ways low confidence can manifest itself in leadership:

- **Physical presentation** – Your posture, the way you stand, the way you dress, self-care habits, physical health, and wellness.

*names are changed to protect confidentiality

- **Communication** – The way you speak to others, the way you respond to criticism, rate of speech, the words you use, and your ability to defend yourself during a confrontation.

- **Inner dialogue** – What you say to yourself when you make a mistake, your ability to accept feedback, how you interpret others' actions or messages, jumping to conclusions, engaging in all-or-nothing thinking, assuming others are "out to get you," and being overly sensitive to how others perceive you.

- **Relationships** – Difficulty trusting others; eagerness to please, and poor boundaries.

Regardless of your past experiences, you *must* do what is necessary to ensure a positive self-image so that you can confidently lead your team to excellence. If you believe in yourself, you will believe in your team. If you believe in your team, they will believe in your leadership, and ultimately, the company's mission.

**6. Focus on employees:** Effective leaders focus on the right things. While their lazy counterparts focus only on profit margins, their board, or their product, skilled leaders focus a lot of their energy on their *employees*. That's right. Employees. Your biggest investors are right there in front you! If you want to be effective in your position, it is critical that you program your mind to focus on the needs of your team members. If you don't spend some time every day thinking about how to improve your relationship with your employees (more on that later) or keep them happy and invested,

*names are changed to protect confidentiality

you are wasting time. Sure, you may argue that without your clients or a good product, you don't have a company, but I contend that it is your *employees* who are in control. It is your *employees* who are keeping the customers happy. It is your *employees* who are staying up late at night working to keep your company running. They spend more time with you and your business than they do with their own families, so *invest in them*. Spend time thinking about their experience and how to keep them. Remember, another company will probably be willing to put them first if you won't.

## Behavior

*Does your behavior match that of a leader who is confident, self-assured, and empowered?*

Well now you look good and have an amazing attitude. That's great, but now you actually have to do the work, you know, be a leader and stuff. As a supervisor, your behavior is being monitored at every moment by your employees. They watch how you work, examine the quality of everything you submit, and look to see whether what you say matches what you do. Let's first discuss all the various facets of communication as it relates to effective leadership. Here we go!

**1. NONVERBAL COMMUNICATION:** Your face, hands, and body communicate something to your audience at all times (even when you don't want them to). They send a message about your values, impressions, likes, dislikes, and overall interest in people

*names are changed to protect confidentiality

and ideas. Remember I said earlier that effective leaders are self-aware? Well, this includes being aware of the nonverbal messages you are sending as well. Have you ever been told that your opinion is "written all over your face?" Do you cross your arms every time you get bad news? Do you clench your fists when you are nervous? This stuff matters!

It's time for an activity. Ready?

I want you to ask the three people closest to you the following question, *"How do you know when I am happy/mad/displeased/nervous, even without me saying a word?"* Listen to the answers very carefully, because whatever you show in your personal life may also be how you show up as a leader. For instance, if your partner tells you that they always know when you're upset because you get quiet and cross your arms, observe if this is something you're doing with your team. If your brother-in-law tells you that you look down when you're nervous, pay attention! There's a chance you might be doing this when you deliver bad news to your team.

Here are some ways to show confidence through nonverbal communication:

- **Walking** – Walk with power and intention. Look straight ahead of you and maintain excellent posture. Maintain a steady pace-not too fast and not too slow. A pace that is too fast makes you look hurried and disorganized. A pace that is too slow makes you seem overly relaxed or even insecure.

*names are changed to protect confidentiality

- **Facial expressions** – Your face can do so many things! Be very aware of what your eyebrows do when you are upset and be careful not to press your lips when you are displeased. Try to develop a "look" that is somewhat natural, yet confident. Maintain a slight smile when listening to others (even if they are irritating the heck out of you) and make sure you are breathing throughout! When engaged in conversation, make sure to maintain eye contact. This alone can help you connect to your audience by showing that you are attentive and engaged in that moment. Strong eye contact sends the message "I'm here with you. You are important. What we are discussing is important." It also sends a message of authority and self-confidence.

- **Eye contact** – Eye contact is particularly important during virtual calls when you don't have the ability to physically connect with the audience. To send a message of confidence and authority, make it a point to speak to the camera (yes, that little circle on your laptop or computer) *directly*. A lot of people struggle with this. Some of my clients have told me that it feels "weird" to speak directly to a camera when they can't see the person there in front of them. So, what do they do? They look down at the person's image or away from the screen altogether. *That's a big mistake.* Looking away, even for a moment, gives your audience permission to disengage. It also doesn't help you look polished or focused. You want your audience's attention *at all times*. Look right into that camera anytime you are speaking. Glance down at your

*names are changed to protect confidentiality

notes briefly if you need to but always focus your attention straight ahead into that little camera.

- **Hands/Feet** – If you are going to present yourself as a confident, self-assured leader, you must maintain proper control of your hands and feet. This means placing your hands on top of the table or your desk during meetings (instead of hiding them underneath). It means making sure not to fidget or play with your nails, watch, or hair. It also means having your feet firmly planted on the floor, making sure not to swivel in your chair (if you're a big kid like me, you know this is hard) or shake your leg uncontrollably. Remember, the idea is to look as relaxed, confident, and in control as you actually are! Movement should be intentional with the purpose of *enhancing* or adding to your message. Anything else is a distraction.

**2. VERBAL COMMUNICATION:** Effective leaders understand how powerful language is and they use it to their advantage. Lazy leaders take language for granted, not understanding that it is a tool for building trust, establishing connections, and building a strong personal brand. Words do, in fact, matter. The words themselves matter. How you relay the message matters. Allow me to provide you with my best tips for communicating like a winner!

- **Pause** – This is huge. Often, people are inclined to respond *immediately* to a question. They *jump* to share their opinion, respond to an email, or correct someone. They don't take a

*names are changed to protect confidentiality

moment to breath before opening their mouth. For someone in a leadership position, impulsivity can be very dangerous. You need to pause before responding (or speaking) to ensure that what you are about to say is 1) really what you want to say, 2) accurate, 3) in line with your personal brand, and 4) in your best interest (and that of the team). Taking that breath before speaking also enables you to look and sound polished, professional, and in control of the situation. In my coaching practice, I have a rule about this. I have my clients count two Mississippi's before speaking or responding to a question. Try it out!

Here's a case example.

One day, I decided to send a motivational email to my coaching client *Charlotte. In it, I included a message on the power of pausing before taking action. About ten minutes after sending the email, I received a message from Charlotte that I'll never forget. It read: "Monica, you just saved my job!" As it turned out, Charlotte was in the middle of writing an angry email to her boss when she read my email. My reminder to *pause* resulted in Charlotte taking a deep breath, stepping away from her desk, and assessing the situation more fully. Charlotte decided against sending that email to her boss, eventually realizing that she was responding "out of anger" instead of thinking rationally.

- **Speak slowly** – We live in an era where everything is rushed and has a deadline. We eat quickly, we speak quickly, and

*names are changed to protect confidentiality

we drive quickly. We rush to our next destination even when we don't have an appointment. Our communication is no different. We race through our message in a manner that is very disorganized, hoping that it makes sense to the receiver. Effective leaders take their time when they speak because they know that *what they have to say is important*. They know that their employees are listening. They know that their words have consequences. They understand that every word matters (and can't be taken back), so they speak with intention.

Lazy leaders are careless with their words. They run their mouth without thinking twice about how their message comes off. Whatever comes out, comes out! You, however, want to come off as polished. You want to be taken seriously. And you want your people to hear every word you say, so that there's no confusion or misunderstanding.

Think about the leaders in your life that you admire. Do they rush through their words or do they speak slowly and with intention? In this discussion, I often bring up former U.S. president Barack Obama as an example. Regardless of political affiliation, most leaders would describe this President as an eloquent speaker. When he speaks, others listen. He knows the *power of words* and the power of his messages, so he uses his time wisely. Go ahead. Go to YouTube and watch some of Obama's speeches and interviews. What you will see is a leader who speaks slowly and carefully because he knows he is worthy of taking up time and space.

*names are changed to protect confidentiality

If you struggle in this area, I encourage you to think about *why* you are rushing through your message. Some of my coaching clients say that they speak quickly when they are nervous. Others say that they rush through their words when they feel insecure or intimidated by their audience. I urge you to figure out where it comes from for *you* and then work hard to improve in this area. Your employees are listening.

- **Word choice** – I said that every word matters, so listen closely. As an effective leader, you must be careful with the words you choose to speak. If you want to be seen as confident and empowered, use language that supports that kind of a personal brand and get rid of language that distracts from your message. First, get rid of *filler words.* You know what these are: the "uhms" and the "you know" and the "uh." The worst one of them all is "so." I hear it all the time. "So the next thing on our agenda is…" or "So in order to proceed with the plan…" *Stop it.*

When lazy leaders communicate, they use filler words because they are nervous, are desperately searching for their next word, or feel insecure about their message. These words are garbage! They serve absolutely no purpose and are making you look insecure and disorganized. Pause in between your thoughts and do not open your mouth until you are ready to deliver your next word/sentence.

The second thing to get rid of is *minimizing language.*

*names are changed to protect confidentiality

## Minimizing language are the words or phrases that serve to "downplay" your message or who you are as a leader.

Examples include, "kind of," "sort of," "maybe," and "perhaps." If you've ever heard someone say at a meeting, "Can I just ask a quick question?" You know how awful it sounds. It might even have been you who said it! To sounds like a confident leader, you need to get rid of these phrases and replace them with language that is strong and affirmative. When giving your opinion on something, consider making statements that begin with, "I suggest" or "I recommend" or "in my experience."

- **Be concise** – In order to be effective in your verbal communication, you must be able to get to your point quickly. Effective leaders know how to avoid rambling. Instead, they choose to be as brief as possible when speaking or responding to someone (this is why pausing and pacing yourself is so important). When I work with my executive coaching clients, I urge them to dig deep and figure out *why* they ramble. Why is it difficult to be concise? Where does this urge to give every possible detail come from??
The psychology of this is important!

There are many reasons why people ramble. It could be that they don't feel secure in what they're saying, so they keep going and going like the energizer bunny, hoping that eventually something they say will make sense. Another possible reason people ramble is

*names are changed to protect confidentiality

because they want to take up as much space as possible. I've worked with a few CEOs who admittedly love to hear themselves talk and will take over a conversation because their ideas are "that great."

If your struggle is connected to feelings of insecurity, I urge you to work through this as soon as possible! Earlier, I indicated that confidence is a key ingredient for effective leadership, so invest in and seek council from a coach, mentor, or trusted person who can help guide you toward a more realistic, positive self-image. If your struggle to speak concisely is connected to feelings of superiority, I urge you to speak to someone who can help you understand where this comes from, so you can develop a less egocentric view of yourself.

An effective leader is the person in the meeting who talks the least.

The next time you are leading a team meeting, take note of how long it takes you to answer a question. Consider how much talking you are doing in comparison to your team members. Control the need to share each and every single thought you have and be selective in what (and how much) you share. Be brief. Ask yourself, "What is the focus/objective here and how can I respond with as few words as possible?" Consider what the other person is really asking you. Once you have answered the question, stop speaking! Less is more, my friends.

- **Ask open-ended questions** – I have worked with hundreds of managers over the years and have seen how incredibly overwhelmed some of them are. They race through their day

*names are changed to protect confidentiality

answering phone calls, returning emails, and completing reports as quickly as humanly possible to meet tight deadlines. When communicating with direct reports, their focus is on one thing – getting what they want.

Lazy leaders are typically linear in their communication, focusing mostly on their needs or end goal. As a result, they answer questions declaratively by simply answering the question or telling the employee what they want (or what's going to happen).

For these lazy leaders, the focus is linear – "I tell *you* what I think, and you take it." An effective leader, by contract, sees communication with a direct report as *transactional*. They make every effort to respond to a question or statement with an open-ended question because they seek information just as much as they give it. Some folks might reject the idea of open-ended questions because they may feel that they "don't have the time to explore the employee's views." They prefer the less time-consuming option of speaking without actually holding a conversation.

**Are you speaking to your employees or are you having *conversations* with them?**

Of course, there will be some instances where a full conversation isn't possible or isn't appropriate. You could be pressed for time, you could be trying to meet a tight deadline, or you could be taking disciplinary action with an employee and need to be direct in your approach. In most, cases, however, open-ended questions

*names are changed to protect confidentiality

can–and should–be used. Resist the temptation to constantly tell employees what to do. Resist the urge to deliver information and then leave. Even when you know what decision you're going to make, stop for a minute and engage in a conversation with your staff. Ask for their opinion. Get their perspective on things and you will find that they have brilliant ideas just waiting to be developed.

Here are some great examples of open-ended questions that serve to empower employees and build relationships:

1. What is working well right now?

2. How can we make this process more efficient?

3. What does success look like for you?

4. What struggles are you having?

5. How can I support you better?

6. How can we take this project to the next level?

7. Based on your experience, what would work best here?

Allow me to share an example of how this would work to show the benefit it has on employee experience. Last year, I was on a coaching call with a client—an HR director for a major university. He shared with me the details of a conversation he was having with a direct report around an issue with a student. My client's immediate response was to simply answer the question and tell the employee what he should do. The direct report acknowledged his boss' response and left the office.

*names are changed to protect confidentiality

What was wrong with this interaction? Seems like a simple, straightforward interaction. A question was asked and an answer was given. This approach would work fine for a lazy leader. However, as an effective leader, you have an opportunity to use open-ended questions to empower the employee and encourage critical thinking. I asked my client (with an open-ended question of course), "How did your employee benefit or grow as a result of your interaction?" My coaching client was confused. I explained that every conversation with a direct report (no matter how small) can turn into an opportunity for growth, self-reflection, and critical thinking. An open-ended question such as, "What are you thinking might be a good approach here?" or "How can we protect both the student and the university in this scenario?" empowers the employee while providing a valuable coaching opportunity.

So, the next time a direct report asks you a question, consider whether it may be helpful to ask an open-ended question instead of quickly handing out a response or making a decision. I know you are busy and want to move on to the next thing on your agenda, but your team members' development is *important*.

- **Come from a place of curiosity** – When communicating with your team, it is often helpful to come from a place of curiosity rather than judgment. Starting your sentences with "I wonder if" or "I wonder how" can encourage critical thinking and prevent you from always coming across as the authority or the only person with all the answers.

*names are changed to protect confidentiality

Consider this scenario. Your direct report walks into your office, frustrated with a fellow colleague. She tells you that she wants your support in confronting the individual regarding recent behavior during team meetings. Instead of responding, "Well, that's not going to work" or "No, I think you should talk to her yourself," you say, "I wonder how that approach would feel to Jennifer. Let's think about the pros and cons of coming at it from this angle." Do you see how different this *feels*? Coming at the situation from a place of curiosity can help diffuse a situation, encourage the employee to explore all possible approaches, and present you as the truly objective party. It also helps to build a relationship with your employee and build *trust*.

- **Listen** – Do you really listen to people when they speak or are you simply hoping they will shut their mouth so you can respond and move on with your day? Most of us are horrible at listening. With the hustle and bustle of our days, we often focus so much on our own needs (our deadlines, our requests, our preferences) that we do not listen to others. Many of us are guilty of this and so are lazy leaders!

In order to be effective, you must learn to shut your mouth and resist the urge to interrupt. Listen to people's (complete) thought, so you can fully understand what they are saying to you. It's important to understand that you are not only listening for content. You are also listening by watching their nonverbal cues, their eyes, their hands, etc. This is *all* a part of listening. Often, your employee will tell you one thing with their words but send a totally

*names are changed to protect confidentiality

different message through their body language. When you focus on both the words and the manner in which the message is delivered, you are much more likely to understand the employee's perspective, convey a message of respect, and behave in ways that are helpful to both parties.

**Listening to others is a requirement for effective leadership. It requires that you pay attention to both content *and* delivery.**

Consider asking yourself the following questions when listening to one of your team members:

1. What is this person trying to convey?

2. What does this person want – for me to listen or for me to do something?

3. What does this person need from me in order to feel supported and heard?

4. How am I demonstrating good listening skills through my nonverbals right now?

5. Is my mind clear, open, and ready to (really) listen to this person's message right now?

- **Identify your (and your employee's) communication style** – One of the biggest mistakes I see my clients make is assuming that everyone on their team communicates and

*names are changed to protect confidentiality

receives information the same way they do. They express a need and then have the nerve to become angry when the other person doesn't respond the way they want them to. This, my friends, is what *managers* do. They adopt a one-size-fits-all approach to work with their team members, refusing to see them as individuals with varying needs, communication styles, and approaches to resolve conflict. Managers are quick to regard team members who are different than them as "difficult" or "oppositional." *Big mistake*. I hate to break it to you, but *you* are the problem here, not them.

A leader understands and appreciates each team member for the unique individual they are. A leader embraces these differences and is able to adjust their approach according to each employee's style. While a manager (lazy leader) is quick to criticize those who are different or dismiss them as being "difficult," a leader recognizes the value in surrounding themselves with people who will challenge their thinking and force them to think outside the box. A leader knows that each team member has something valuable to contribute to the group and gets excited when it brings about healthy conflict and ultimately, amazing new ideas!

The DISC personality profile © offers an exciting way to get to know your team members by identifying four major communication styles. The tool has been amazingly helpful in my work as an executive coach by providing supervisors at all levels with a framework for understanding themselves and those around them.

*names are changed to protect confidentiality

In order to be effective as a leader, you must familiarize yourself with each style and learn how to work with each communication style accordingly. If you don't, you will continue to treat everyone around you the same, with a false expectation that they respond the way *you* want them to. The result? A ton of frustration, anger, and confusion. You will likely also view yourself as a victim instead of a strong, capable leader.

Let's take a look at each of these communication styles right now. As I go over each of them, think about which style you relate to the most. Ready?

- **Dominance (D)** – The first major communication style described by the DISC personality profile is the dominance style. This type of person is generally direct, blunt, and straight to the point. They like to communicate their thoughts in a manner that is concise and tend to look for immediate solutions to problems. The dominant communicator can jump from one thought to the next with ease. They don't have time for excuses or long-winded explanations and become agitated by people who speak very slowly or think long and hard before answering questions. The dominance style is generally intelligent, capable, and a "doer." Communicating with the dominant personality type requires some planning. You must approach them only when you are ready to provide answers, solutions, or recommendations. Conversations should be structured, and your thoughts organized. The dominant communicator

*names are changed to protect confidentiality

simply does not have the time or energy to sit and watch you "figure it all out" in your head. They expect you to come to them with ready to go, concrete information. Want to piss off a dominant personality type? Schedule meetings where you sit and "brainstorm" ideas through long-winded, vague conversation.

Okay, so what's so great about the dominant leader? I'll tell you. A dominant leader is great at being decisive. They get things done. When they commit to an idea, project, or position, they stand by it and can be relentless in their pursuits. If a team struggles with decision making or taking action, bring in a D-style leader to do what he does best: take action.

*Case example:* A coaching client came to me, frustrated with her boss. She explained that every week she would prepare a detailed progress report to be shared with her supervisor during their weekly one on one. During these meetings, my client's boss would interrupt her as she tried to share her progress report. She would take over the conversation and end the meeting early. My client felt invisible. She felt as though her boss didn't care about her projects or value her time. I asked my coaching client whether this progress report was something her boss asked her to create. Apparently, it was not. My client, thinking that her boss would appreciate a detailed update report, took the initiative to create the report. And here we have it! Two different communication styles bumping heads with one another. My client's boss has a dominant communication/leadership style. My client, not knowing this,

*names are changed to protect confidentiality

communicated and behaved in a way that felt natural for her. *Big mistake.* I helped my client understand that her boss was not, in fact, a jerk. She was simply communicating as a true D-style leader. My client's detailed progress reports were seen more as a nuisance instead of a tool. Her long-winded explanations were anything but helpful and her sharing of details was deemed to be unnecessary. I worked with my client, so she could adjust her personal communication style to match that of her boss more closely. She got rid of the notes and allowed her D-style boss to take the lead in their 1:1 meetings. She focused on delivering information in a manner that was very high level and direct. Finally, if there were any details she really wanted to share with her boss, she shared them after the meeting via email. The result? Their relationship blossomed and the 1:1 meetings became more enjoyable and productive for both parties.

*How to approach your dominance style employee:* If you have a dominance style individual on your team, make sure you keep your conversation short and sweet. When delivering bad news, be direct and tell it like it is. They will appreciate that. Avoid the tendency to give them long, drawn out instructions (as they would prefer to figure it out on their own anyway). Put your dominance style employee in situations where they can lead others and exercise some independence. Need something done right away? Go to your dominance team member. Need someone to step up and take lead on a project? Your dominance employee is the one to go to.

*Email tips:* When communicating with the dominance style employee via email, get right to the point and keep your message short. No need to start the email with pleasantries or a detailed

*names are changed to protect confidentiality

background of the problem. Give the dominance team member what they need to get the job done and get out of their way!

> ▶ **Influence (I)** – The second major communication style as described by the DISC personality profile is the influence or interpersonal type. This communicator is primarily driven by relationships or connections with other people. They are friendly, outgoing, and enthusiastic about the work they do. The influence type is motivated by a need to entertain or charm others. They like to be liked and see their team as one big family. At an extreme, the influence type can focus too much on relationships and not enough on business, the "big picture," or accuracy of work. In order to work effectively with the influence type, effective leaders must provide regular opportunities for working with others. Show enthusiasm, engage in (appropriate) personal conversation, and be friendly. Finally, communicate (and explain things) in a way that is "big picture" focused. Avoid focusing too much on detail. Instead, think impact, both long and short term. This will go a long way with the influence type.

What's so great about an influence type leader? Easy! They get people excited about their work and the vision. They have amazing ideas and are great "outside of the box" thinkers. If your team has lost its spunk and is in need of a fresh energy to get them going, bring in an influence style leader to remind them of why they do the work that they do.

*names are changed to protect confidentiality

*Case example:* I once had an employee named *Carol who was a high I. She was super friendly and a joy to be around. The team loved her because she took an interest in their personal lives and was very understanding. One day during a team meeting, Carol's colleagues started complaining about a system that was recently put in place. It was innovative and would make everyone's lives easier. You could feel the excitement in the air. "I *love* that idea," they said. The conversation continued on to other topics and Carol's recommendation was never put into fruition.

What went wrong here? I'll tell you. Carol had a great idea. Everyone got excited. No one did anything. Carol, as an influence type, is not naturally driven to lay out a plan of action for her plans. Her style lends itself only to thinking outside the box and *generating* the idea. As a leader, I had to figure out what to do here.

I had a couple of options. First, I could adapt my style in order to support Carol's idea. This would mean meeting her halfway by joining in her excitement and asking her clarifying questions so that we could figure out *how* to make her idea a reality. Another option (I prefer this one because it calls on the strengths of the entire team) is to call upon another team member (preferably someone who is detail oriented and logical) to "take the baton" after the idea has been presented. This individual would take Carole's idea and identify the steps necessary for making it happen. This would include who does what and by when. There you have it! We are working as a team and I, as the leader, was assigning tasks according to individual strengths.

*names are changed to protect confidentiality

*How to approach your influence style employee:* To enjoy a good relationship with your influence style team member, bring out your friendly side and don't shy away from (appropriate) personal conversations. Before jumping into business, ask them how their weekend was or how their son's basketball game went. Listen to them and don't be afraid to share a little about yourself during a conversation. Need someone to build a relationship with a new client? The influence employee is your guy! Need someone to serve on a committee to discuss a big, new idea? Your influence employee should be considered first.

*Email tips:* Your influence style team member needs you to say hello before jumping into business on an email. Start messages with pleasantries and stay focused on the big picture. Avoid making your email super short as this employee might see you as cold or detached this way. Your influence style employee needs to understand why you're doing something so stay focused on the mission, vision, and overall goals. Focus on impact. Once they see *why* something is important, they will be all in.

> ▶ **Steady (S)** – The third major communication style is the steady type. This person prefers to find ways to keep people happy and feeling good. As a person who values the group dynamic, they approach others with caution as they are concerned with how others will perceive them and relate to them. They are sensitive to criticism and judgement. They take their time when communicating and do not feel the urge to rush through their message.

*names are changed to protect confidentiality

Deadlines are not something they particularly value. When communicating with the steady communicator type, it's important to take your time and give this team member your undivided attention. Choose your words carefully to avoid a misunderstanding and avoid speaking too quickly. Check in periodically throughout the conversation to make sure that your employee is okay and taking in everything you are saying. Give the steady type time to ask questions before, during, and after your exchange. The thing to remember here is *slow and steady*.

*Case example*: I once had an employee named *Maria who was a strong steady type communicator. Maria was incredibly loyal, kind, and trustworthy. Everyone loved her! At the time, I had a strong dominant style of communication (you can imagine how this is going to go). Whenever I would meet with Maria, I would find myself frustrated by her slow and steady style. If I asked her something like "How did the meeting go?" I was met with an (extra) long pause and an even longer answer. To me, it felt like I could go to lunch and come back, and Maria would still be in the middle of finishing her sentence. I was ready *to pull my hair out*!

As I developed as a leader and became more intentional in approaching each team member according to their individual style, my attitude changed. I realized that Maria was not the problem. I was! If I wanted Maria to be productive and flourish in her role, I had to adjust to her style and quickly. First, I changed my mindset. I committed myself to slowing down my speech and my overall

*names are changed to protect confidentiality

delivery when meeting with Maria. I scheduled 1:1s on days when my schedule was not full, and I could afford to take an extra minute to chat. During our conversations, I made sure to give Maria my *undivided* attention – no multitasking or checking emails. I added some strategic pauses throughout as I spoke to Maria and made sure to talk about one topic or request at a time.

What happened over time was amazing. I found myself to be more centered during our conversations. I was less impatient (gotta love the dominance style) and more open to Maria's ideas because my mind wasn't focused on moving to the next thing. Because of my ability to adjust my natural style, Maria and I developed a more constructive and trusting relationship.

*How to approach your steady style employee:* The steady style employee wants you to take your time and connect with them as human beings before jumping into business. To build a strong relationship with the steady style, you will need to speak slowly and focus your energy on making them comfortable. Avoid cutting a meeting short if you can, as this might make them feel that you don't care about them. For 1:1s, allow a little extra time to meet with the steady style employee. Include an agenda to keep them on track as they can sometimes lose focus or take a while getting to their point. For this reason, you should set clear deadlines for the steady style and check in on their progress regularly. They need and want your support. Need some ideas for improving morale on the team? The steady employee is the one to ask. Need someone to mentor the new guy and make him feel welcome? The steady will be perfect for this.

*names are changed to protect confidentiality

*Email tips:* When emailing the steady style...just kidding. Do *not* email the steady employee unless you have to. As emotional beings, the steady prefers a face-to-face connection over any other type of communication. If this is not possible, I recommend picking up the phone and calling your steady person directly. If an email is necessary (and in many cases it will be), be sure to start with pleasantries and/or a *sincere* statement of appreciation for something they did. It doesn't matter if what they did is small, it's more about the gesture than anything else. In your email to the steady employee, you're going to also want to keep it simple. Avoid giving more than two directives in one email, as this can cause them to feel overwhelmed. Keep it simple: statement of appreciation + simple directive + deadline = success. I know this might seem like a lot of work, but this is how you set up the steady person for success.

▸ **Conscientious (C)** – The fourth major communication style, as outlined by DISC is the *conscientious* style. This type of employee has a preference for order and structure. They communicate in a manner that is supported by facts, data, and logic. If your argument doesn't make sense or isn't well thought out, this type of employee will reject it. The conscientious style may not be great at making immediate decisions or forming strong emotional bonds with coworkers. They would rather focus on the work, making sure that all is precise, and above all, *accurate*. When meeting with the conscientious communicator, make sure you are prepared and organized. Take your time when speaking (beware dominant style!) and do not rush through

*names are changed to protect confidentiality

content. Abide by company rules and be ready to refer to a policy, guideline, or procedure. Leave emotion at the door. Stick to the facts.

*Case example:* I once worked with a young man named *John. John was a high C – detailed, focused, and obsessed with order. He and I initially bumped heads because I found him to be too rigid. John wanted everything his way and by "his way" I mean perfect and without error. And believe me, if there was an error (no matter how small), John would find it. During meetings, he would call people out if they made a mistake and he never, ever forgave them for it.

I can remember telling my own coach at the time, "I don't like him. Actually, I can't stand him!" (By the way, it's okay not to like some of your employees. What matters is that you treat them fairly and with respect.) I knew that if I was going to work with John, I would need to make some changes. I decided that in order to build a stronger relationship with him, I would need to make sure that I was intentional in my work and my communication. I took my time when writing him an email and made sure to triple check my work for accuracy. When communicating with John verbally, I spoke more slowly to give him time to process and made sure not to jump to the next topic without making sure that he had gathered all the facts he needed in order to proceed.

Wow! After taking this new approach for a few weeks, I found that John was less critical of my leadership and seemed more open to my suggestions and directives. He started to trust my judgement

*names are changed to protect confidentiality

more and even appeared more relaxed during our 1:1 meetings. Eventually, I even came to like the guy.

*How to approach our conscientious style employee:* The conscientious employee wants you to approach them with *facts*. Do your research and be ready to provide answers to their potential questions. Since this type of person values order, be sure to keep your promises and go by the book with them. If your meeting with them is scheduled for one o'clock, make sure you're ready to begin at one o'clock. Showing up late to meetings, arriving unprepared, and beating around the bush are all ways to push the conscientious employee away. Be direct, speak slowly, and most of all, be precise! Believe me, if you make a mistake, they will find it so cross your Ts and dot your Is.

*Email tips:* Your email message to a conscientious employee should be well-structured and well thought out. Be sure to review your message several times before sending to ensure that all information is accurate and clear. Make sure to lay everything out step by step and avoid using vague language. Trust me, nothing pisses off a conscientious person more than errors or what they perceive to be a lack of attention to detail. If you're not sure about something you're writing, *do not make it up* and do not guess. Be direct, clear, and super organized.

A supervisor's ability to communicate with their staff according to their individual style is critical to the team's success. While the lazy leader communicates in a manner that feels natural and easy, the effective leader will go through a process of self-discovery which requires that they first identify their own natural style. This

*names are changed to protect confidentiality

can be done independently or with assistance from a coach who can provide the necessary diagnostic tools for self-identification. Once this is done and you understand the good, the bad, and the ugly of your natural style, it will be time to identify your employees' communication style. This will take some work but ultimately your job will be to tweak your own style to match that of your team member more closely. This might mean that with John you need to be clearer and more direct. It might mean that with Sweta you need to build a more personal connection. It might mean that with George you need to be more big-picture focused. And it might mean that with Helen you need to slow your speech and focus more on facts than on opinion. Get it? This is not about *changing* who you are. It's about making adjustments so that you meet each person halfway.

**3. OWNING MISTAKES** – Be quick to apologize, quick to forgive, and quick to admit when you don't know something.

A lazy leader is proud and unable (or unwilling) to admit when they are wrong. They see apologies as a sign of weakness and fear losing control. An effective leader, by contract, can acknowledge mistakes quickly. They don't take things personally but rather, focus on how to correct the error and move forward. They know that honesty goes a long way and that apologizing with sincerity (and with a plan of action) builds relationships with those they need the most. Now, let me be clear. Effective leaders are capable of acknowledging their mistakes, but they do so in a manner that does not compromise their authority or tarnish their personal brand. They acknowledge the error and then they apologize once,

*names are changed to protect confidentiality

*only once*. Over apologizing can make you look insecure, so only one genuine, clear apology is necessary. If your employee is the one who made the mistake or treated you unfairly, it is your duty as an effective leader to immediately forgive that person (with or without the apology). Forgiveness can mean accepting the apology and moving on. It could also mean accepting that the person may not be remorseful at all and choosing to focus on the business without hurt feelings or a grudge that lasts six months. Behave like the emotionally mature adult that you are! Remember that you are there to perform the duties assigned to your role, not pout like a six-year-old whose best friend took her cookies at lunch.

**Leaders don't know everything, and that's okay.**

It's important to apologize when needed and forgive quickly when others make mistakes, but it is also critical to admit when you don't know something. I'll let you in on a secret. It is *impossible* for any leader to know *everything* and have all the answers. Lazy leaders will pretend to know everything because (again, the ego is at play) and there's a fear of "looking dumb." Let me tell you what is truly dumb. Dumb is giving false information to a direct report because you don't know the answer. Dumb is speaking aimlessly for 15 minutes about something you don't know, thinking that the more you speak, the more convincing you will be. There is nothing polished or professional about this. You are better off telling your team that you don't know the answer and then share your (specific) plan to follow up with the information requested. Trust me, you

*names are changed to protect confidentiality

can say, "I don't know, but I will commit to getting that answer for you" with confidence and polish. Your credibility is at stake here so be careful!

**4. PERFORMANCE** – As a leader, you need to perform at a high level, so that others can be inspired and follow your example. Failing to perform at an optimal level can put your credibility at risk which will create a divide between you and your team. Let's take a closer look at the different facets of performance as it relates to effective leadership.

- **Quality** – Remember your first day on the job? You were so excited to start fresh and make a great impression. You put your all into every project, every report, and every email communication. You gave 110% into everything you did. What happened?? For many lazy leaders, this passion for excellence fades once they feel comfortable and "safe" in their new role. They start to get lazy and it shoes in everything they do. Can you relate? For you, this may have happened a few months into your role or perhaps even a few years.

In order to be effective, you must go above and beyond with every single thing that has your name attached to it. Anything less than 100 percent effort is considered mediocrity, and this is unacceptable. Do I expect perfection? No, I expect you to perform at a level that is truly and honestly your *best*. Nothing less. Making

*names are changed to protect confidentiality

excuses for why you couldn't give it your all? Welcome to the lazy leader club.

Do me a favor and take out the last report or project you submitted. Hold it up high in front of you. Look at it and ask yourself whether you put your all into it. Your answer will be an indication of how seriously you take your role as a leader.

Here are the top two excuses I hear my coaching clients make for submitting work that is mediocre (along with my responses):

- "I didn't have enough time." (Did you manage your time effectively? Did you make this a priority?)

- "I didn't understand what was being asked of me." (Did you schedule a time with your boss to discuss the expected outcome? Did you ask for help or further clarification or did you assume you would figure it out?)

- **Consistency** – As an effective leader, you must perform at an optimal level. This amazing quality of work must be consistent, though, if you want to be amazing. You absolutely cannot fluctuate between outstanding performance and mediocre performance. That is *not* excellence, my friends. Sorry to break it to you but the day you signed on to be a leader, you also inadvertently agreed to take this on full time. Not when you "feel like it" or "when it is easy." You must outperform your predecessor in order to take your team to new levels of success, so brace yourself for some

*names are changed to protect confidentiality

hard work. This means understanding that there is no "break" from leadership.

Remember, your team is watching your every move, so make sure that your effort and energy levels are high, even when others have lost their zest.

- **Meeting deadlines/punctuality** – If you are to set an example to your team, it is imperative that you respect people's time and honor deadlines. Make sure to submit projects and respond to others on time (if not ahead of schedule). Don't be the type of manager (or lazy leader) who gives other people deadlines but feels they can hand stuff in whenever they feel like it because of their position. Whatever you would expect from a direct report is the *exact same thing* you should strive for.

Let me ask you, if a team meeting starts at nine in the morning, what time would you plan to arrive or log in? I hope the answer is by a quarter to nine. Why so early, you ask? Arriving to your meeting early gives you time to prepare or respond to anything that might go wrong. If you're having technical difficulties, this buffer gives you time to contact IT or restart your computer. If you forget to send out a meeting invite, this allows you the time to send one out. Arriving early to a meeting also gives you time to prepare mentally. Use this time to review your notes or go over any action items from your last meeting. You can also choose to engage with

*names are changed to protect confidentiality

other team members who arrive to the meeting early (what a great opportunity to build relationships!).

> **Arriving early allows your team to see you as a leader who takes them (and the information to be discussed) seriously.**

Arrive early. Be prepared.

Get yourself centered mentally and in the role of an amazing leader. Do this consistently and require that others do the same. In the space of respecting people's time, you also want to make sure you end meetings (in person or in the virtual space) on time. This sends the message that you regard everyone's time as valuable, not just yours.

There is no such thing as a "break" from effective leadership. Take your role seriously and perform at high levels all the time, not just when you feel like it.

## Relationships

*Does the quality of your relationships match that of leader who is confident, self-assured, and empowered?*

Every single well-respected leader who has been regarded as effective understands that they cannot become excellent by themself. To be excellent, a leader needs to identify, develop, and maintain strong personal and professional relationships. They need to

*names are changed to protect confidentiality

understand that individual success is a group effort and should be taken seriously.

Lazy leaders don't need anyone. They have an I'll-do-it-myself attitude and regard others as either competitors or intruders. Lazy leaders don't see the value in fostering meaningful relationships, be it with other people or other businesses. They may have learned that people are "not to be trusted" or that in life you must "only look out for yourself." In some cases, these managers don't completely isolate themselves. They surround themselves with other people, but these individuals may be destructive, envious, or professionally stagnant. Both situations are equally dangerous.

Let's stop for a moment to do an exercise. Below, write down the names of the five people you spend the most time with. Next to each person's name, describe how that individual supports you or makes you better as a person or professional.

Person 1 _____

How he/she supports me _____

Person 2 _____

How he/she supports me _____

Person 3 _____

How he/she supports me _____

Person 4 _____

How he/she supports me _____

*names are changed to protect confidentiality

Person 5 _____

How he/she supports me _____

Look at your list. What this exercise difficult? Do you have any blanks next to people's names? I hope not. If you have people around you who are not contributing to your happiness or professional success, why are they there??

I can remember facilitating a leadership workshop a while back where I had participants try this exercise. One woman–a mid-level executive–approached me after class, looking for some guidance. She explained that she couldn't think of anything to put down next to her husband's name. The woman went on to share that her husband "really didn't support her in any way." She laughed and added, "Really, he gets in the way because he doesn't like my job and never supports me when I want to take a class or improve myself in some way."

Can you imagine what I was thinking as I was listening to this woman? I waited until she was done sharing and then I immediately asked, "If your husband doesn't support you in any way, why are you still with him?" Her response was simply, "Because he's my husband." I'll spare you the rest of our conversation, but I let her know that this was deeply concerning to me. The fact that she (continues to) allows anyone in her life who does nothing for her personal or professional growth is astounding. I know some people will disagree with me but think about it! In order to be effective leaders (or simply the best version of ourselves), we need to think of ourselves as a *business*. This means that we must intentionally set

*names are changed to protect confidentiality

ourselves up for success and we must *surround ourselves* with only the best. I understand that people are not perfect. I understand that we all make mistakes. But in order to be excellent, we need people around us who will motivate and inspire us (in some way) to reach our greatest potential.

Each and every one of us needs other people to achieve excellence. We need their support, their money, their expertise, and their time. We need someone to bounce ideas of off –people to tell us when we are wrong and motivate us to get back on track. We need to *surround ourselves with excellence*. Look at the people you have allowed into your personal space. Do they belong there? Do they *deserve* to be there? I understand that it may be difficult (or even heartbreaking) to remove family members or longtime friends from your life.

**Please understand that you can love or respect people from a distance.**

Rip the band-aid off. Cut the cord. Life is too damn short to keep people around for them to just "be there." Your life is a business and the people around you serve as your personal board of directors so make smart decisions.

For the effective leader, professional relationships are critical. They help determine your level of success in many ways. If you are the type of person who believes they can make it on their own, it's time to reconsider this approach. Professional relationships, when maintained and nurtured, can help improve your confidence,

*names are changed to protect confidentiality

encourage diversity in thought, and open up opportunities for growth and advancement. The effective leader recognizes this fact and never takes a single relationship for granted.

The first step in excelling in this area (the fourth and final area identified in my Wheel of Excellence model) is to identify the right relationships. What industry are you in? Marketing? Banking? Pharma? Education? Every industry has people who are highly regarded in their field, considered to be influential in some way. These are the "go-to" people in your industry. It could be an author who has written books on a subject matter in your field. It could be the president of your company. It could be someone you respect on your team. *Find these people.* You don't have to know them personally (yet). Just find out who they are and make a list of their names.

Now that you have identified key people in your industry or business, it's time to develop relationships with them. If these people work with you, reach out via email (or in person). Invite them to lunch or for a quick coffee. At the very least, introduce yourself. See if you can volunteer to join their committee or resource group. Many companies have clubs or groups that you can join, so get active! Another way to connect is through LinkedIn. Do a search for the people you've identified on your list and send them a connection request. Then, build the relationship! Endorse them for skills, like and comment on their posts, or send them a private message. If your person is an author, speaker, or presenter, attend their events and introduce yourself after their talk or presentation. Do whatever is necessary to connect.

*names are changed to protect confidentiality

The third step is to nurture your relationship. Many of my coaching clients excel at identifying and building relationships but they miss that critical third piece – *nurturing* the relationship. Listen to me. You cannot do all the work of finding and connecting with amazing people only to leave them alone after that. For those of you who have children, think about this: after conceiving and giving birth to your baby, is the job of parenting complete? No. You have to then help the child develop, mature, and grow into an amazing human being. This is also the case with relationships. It takes a certain level of commitment and consistency to nurture your professional relationships. Ask yourself, "When was the last time I checked in x?" or "How can I support y?" Remember, building relationships can also mean asking others if they need help. Pay attention to what your key people are working on and find ways to show them support. Below are some ideas for how you, my effective leader, can nurture your relationships:

- Invite your key person to lunch or coffee.

- Check in with your key person via email.

- Ask your key person how you can help with their project or assigned task.

- Support your key person on social media by liking and commenting on their posts.

- Attend your key person's events or speaking engagements. Share their posts!

*names are changed to protect confidentiality

- Write a review of your key person's work/product/book/research on the internet.

- Volunteer to speak at your key person's event or join their steering committee.

- Publicly acknowledge your key person at a meeting or via a group email.

These are only a few, easy ways to nurture key professional relationships. Make sure that when you do engage or offer assistance, it is done in a manner that is genuine and supportive. Never do something out of obligation or just to get on someone's good side. The goal is to develop a mutually beneficial relationship based on respect that can be sustained over the years.

## Building Relationships with Your Team Members

Building relationships that will benefit you professionally is nice. Building relationships with your direct reports is *required* and should be regarded as a top priority, regardless of the industry you're in. Let's start from the beginning. Your relationship with a team member begins the moment you join the team or the moment they join the team. It is at the moment that you set the precedent for what the employee can expect from you, and ultimately, whether or not you are to be *trusted* as a supervisor.

The first thing you want to do to develop a positive relationship with your team member is to present yourself in a manner

*names are changed to protect confidentiality

that is open and genuine. Your employees are naturally going to be curious about you. They will be asking themselves, "Who is she?" "Where did she come from?" "Does she know what she's doing?" "Is she going to make us do more work?" or "Can I trust her?" It is okay to answer some personal questions but be selective when doing so. Feel free to share a bit about your kids, your hobbies, or travel experiences. Do *not* share anything about your love life, political views, religious views, or feelings about previous employers. Keep it light, keep it friendly, and keep it professional. Your team members don't need to know everything about you. They just need enough to see that you are a human being, that you are here with good intentions, that you have confidence, and that you are trustworthy.

The next thing you want to do is get to know your team members. As soon as possible, meet with each individual direct report (preferably in person but virtually is okay too). Ask them questions about themselves, their role, and their experiences. Ask them what they like about their job and what they like the least. Do this in a manner that feels welcoming, not threatening. Instead of bombarding them with a scripted list of questions, allow the questions to come naturally in the form of a conversation. Above all, be genuine.

## What is your employee's "thing?"

One of the best things you can do is figure out what each person's "thing" is. What do I mean by "thing?" Every single one of us has something (outside of work) that we are passionate about. This can be sports, humanitarian work, cooking, family, fitness, etc.

*names are changed to protect confidentiality

Many years ago, I had a direct report named "Greg." Greg was a great employee and a good person. He coached his son's high school basketball team and spent every single weekend traveling to his games. You could see Greg's face light up every time he talked about his son and his most recent game. He loved everything about the sport and took great joy in helping his son become a great player. Knowing this about Greg, I made sure to regularly check in with him to ask about his son and their latest game. This really shaped our relationship and let him know that I care about him, not only as a professional but also as a human being. Caution: do not use this technique if you cannot be genuine. If you don't really care about the person's "thing," don't mention it. You will do more damage this way.

## Activity

Stop what you're doing right now and write down the names of three of your employees. Next to their names, write down at least one of their favorite hobbies or interests – something they are passionate about! This could include their favorite football team, their passion for gardening, or their devotion to animal rights. Go ahead, I'll wait...

**Employee #1**

Name _____

Has a passion for _____

*names are changed to protect confidentiality

**Employee #2**

Name _____

Has a passion for _____

**Employee #3**

Name _____

Has a passion for _____

If this exercise was difficult for you, it means that you have been operating as a lazy leader and not as an effective leader. It means that you are focusing only on outcomes and not paying enough attention to the people helping you achieve those goals. Starting today, pay attention to your team and *invest* in them, not just for the work they can do for you but for the human beings that they are.

A few other things are important for you know if you're going to be a leader who has strong relationships with their staff. Start collecting this information as soon as you begin the relationship and revise it over time. This includes:

- Your employee's motivation (reason) for staying with the company.

- Your employee's top three strengths/areas of expertise.

*names are changed to protect confidentiality

- Your employee's preference for how they prefer to be acknowledged (public praise, monetary rewards, opportunities to lead, etc.).

- Your employee's career goals.

You will also want to add a list of situations where the employee shines as well as the environments where they struggle.

Sounds like a lot of work, doesn't it? Well, welcome to leadership! When employees see that you've taken the time to know them, to *really* know them, they will understand that they matter to you. When they know that they matter, they will be more likely to take your lead and execute to the best of their ability.

The next step in building a strong relationship with your team members is trusting them. Give each member of your team the space to be excellent on their own! Trust that they know what they are doing and avoid micromanaging them. You do not need to know what they are doing every minute of the day. Focus on the bigger picture instead. There may come a time when you do need to look more closely at an employee's work for performance issues but approach the situation assuming that the team member knows what they are doing. Trust me, they will appreciate it.

Once trust is built, the next step is to hold the employee accountable. Each team member must know what is expected of them and how their success will be measured. These are conversations that should be happening on a regular basis with the employee taking the lead. Establish clear goals with measurable targets that

*names are changed to protect confidentiality

make use of each person's individual talents. Once these are identified and laid out in written form, schedule regular 1:1 meetings to determine progress toward goals and identify opportunities to extend support where needed. Your team member should *never* feel alone in this process. This is a joint effort between two professionals who want to achieve the company's mission and uphold its values.

Building a relationship with your direct report requires honesty, respect, and flexibility. There is no magic potion for getting along with your team members. It's about listening more than speaking and tailoring your approach to meet their individual needs, communication style, and priorities. At the end of the day, it really is about treating people the way you want to be treated and having their back!

Why is trust important? Can't we just focus on helping people do their job? Why do we need them to trust us? Can't we just focus on having them do their job? The answer is *no*. Trust helps to determine whether a team member will go the extra mile for you. Trust will empower an employee to think outside the box and bring forth new, innovative ideas to the company. Trust will keep an employee there when you are forced to cut salaries or increase workload. It is what you need as a leader in order to go from good to excellent. Without it, you will *never* have a strong team. You will *never* gain your employees' respect. Without trust, you will remain a lazy leader.

Here are some additional tips for gaining trust from your staff:

*names are changed to protect confidentiality

- **Invest in their development** – Employees trust leaders who invest in them. While the lazy leader puts all their time and resources into activities that will improve the bottom line, the effective leader *prioritizes* learning and development. They know that investing in their biggest investors (employees) is a smart business move because a happy employee is a productive employee. So, if your employee comes to you and asks if you will pay for them to attend a work-related conference, *do it*. If they ask you to cover the cost of an executive coach, so that they can work on their communication skills, *do it*. Build this into your budget, so that you don't have to worry about where the money will come from. Investing in your people builds trust because it sends the message that their development matters.

- **Be transparent** – Trust is gained when we can be open and honest with our employees. No one is going to trust a supervisor who hides information or keeps secrets. When your staff is kept in the dark, they are indirectly being given the permission to jump to conclusions and create their own narrative about what might be going on. This is so dangerous! Get into the practice of letting your team in on as much as possible. Knowing what is going on with the department and the company makes people feel safe, respected, and appreciated. Some of you may think that your employees don't want to hear about the company's financial troubles or the merger you are considering, but that's not the case at all. Transparency means being honest with employees

*names are changed to protect confidentiality

about the good, the bad, and the scary. You don't need to control everything!

Now, I do understand that there are instances where sharing information with everyone may be damaging or inappropriate. In those situations, I advise you to think carefully about what you can and cannot share. In these cases, share what you can and then *acknowledge* what it is that you cannot share and *why*. Follow up with a (genuine) statement about how the news might make them feel. Offer a safe space for asking questions and always offer yourself for 1:1 time for those who are more private. Remember to *always* frame your language around how the information/decisions will affect your team. *This* is what they want to hear about the most, so address these things head on. (Most staff will wonder whether the change will affect their pay, their responsibilities, their hours, or their resources).

The conversation may sound something like,

"I want to share that we have been discussing the possibility of a merger. We believe that this will be a good business decision for the company for xyz reason(s). Although I am not legally able to reveal the names of the companies we are in discussions with, I can assure you that at this stage, your jobs will not be affected. Should that change, a follow-up discussion will take place well in advance. I understand that this can feel scary and make some people anxious. I want to acknowledge those feelings and answer as many questions as I can, either in this group setting or privately.

*names are changed to protect confidentiality

You are all important to me so you have my word that I will be as straightforward as possible."

When it comes to transparency, it's important to note how damaging it can be for productivity and morale to hide information that others are seeking out. When there is an elephant in the room, address it as quickly as possible. Do not ignore it, try to change the subject, or cover it up. Be brave. Be a leader.

Along with transparency comes the ability to be open about your feelings. Effective leaders know that employees trust a boss who can acknowledge feelings of fear, worry, confusion, and sadness. They understand that this allows others to see you as a strong person, a human being just like them! Lazy leaders hide their feelings out of fear that they will be seen as "weak" or "lacking authority." They walk around like robots focusing only on numbers, data, and the bottom line.

Now, a word of caution. Showing human emotion does not mean that you should cry to your employee because you've had a rough day. It does not mean that you share the details of your divorce during a team meeting and then talk about how depressed you've been. It does not mean that you allow yourself to have a panic attack before a big presentation. It *does mean* that you show emotion in situations where it would help your team relate to you, motivate others, or make you look more human. Be extremely careful about when, where, how, and *to whom* you express emotion. At the end of the day, you are *still* their leader, the person they look up to when they feel hopeless. Your direct reports *should never* have to comfort you. Even when expressing emotion, follow up with a

*names are changed to protect confidentiality

positive statement of hope or potential resolution. Show that no matter what, things will be okay! You will be okay!

Some examples of appropriate expression include:

- You find out that your entire department may be laid off. You share with your team that you "are also scared but feel confident that the company will do what is best for both business and employees."

- You are in a 1:1 meeting with a direct report discussing their recent poor performance. You have repeatedly identified areas for growth and provided support over the last six months with no resolve. They offer nothing during the meeting except a blank look and an "I'm not sure what to tell you." You share with the employee that you feel "frustrated" by her response/lack of progress and will need some time to identify next steps.

- You come back from medical leave after undergoing a serious medical operation. Your employees welcome you with a big party. During a conversation, you admit having felt "overwhelmed and scared" prior to the surgery but are "grateful and relieved" to be back on your feet.

*names are changed to protect confidentiality

- **Keep your promises** – Nothing breaks trust more than making a promise and not following through. Think about it. How would your child feel if you promised to take them out to a movie but then when the day came you gave him an excuse for not going? What if this became a pattern? Over time, your promises would fall on deaf ears. The same is true of your relationship with your employees. When you keep the promises you make, you send a message of trust. When you continuously break your promises, you send a message of disrespect. Sure, there will be times when you're unable to follow through on a promise due to circumstances outside of your control. This alone does not make you a lazy leader. Trouble only comes when you make promises prematurely or fail to offer an explanation for why you can't follow through with the promise. Let's break these down. As an effective leader, it is your job to pause before making promises to your employees. Think things through carefully. Do your research. Go through the necessary channels before making an announcement. Your reputation is on the line! Don't promise to raise salaries if there is a chance it might not happen. Don't promise to increase someone's budget for a project if you haven't received approval from your own supervisor yet. Avoid the urge to make a promise just to look good or make someone like you. This is not about you! If you, for whatever reason, need to break a promise, communicate with the employee or team as soon as possible. I cannot stress this enough! You do not want your people to hear bad news from someone else and certainly don't

*names are changed to protect confidentiality

want to allow time for rumors to start circulating. Nip this in the bud by attacking it head on. Meet with your people, be transparent about what is happening, and share how you plan to address the issue. This is all they want – transparency and a plan.

- **Allow time for fun** – A great way to build trust amongst team members and create a positive workplace culture is to allow time for fun. Now, I obviously am not suggesting that we let folks play games online all day. Nor am I recommending that we have parties at the office 4 days a week. What I am suggesting, is that we encourage our employees to find moments throughout the day where they can laugh, smile, and engage with one another while they do their best work. If you're thinking, "This will get in the way of work!" then you're wrong. A truly effective team will be able to perform at even higher levels when given the space to be silly or joyful throughout the day. Here's an example: I once worked for a company where many of its employees sat in cubicles. My office had glass windows and was situated directly in front of a row of about 10 cubicles. Although this group was with a different department, they were friendly and often engaged me in conversation. One day, one of the employees spontaneously started a game of "catch" with a large ball made of rubber bands. The ball went up and down the row to each employee. Whoever dropped the ball would have to buy lunch for the group the next day. I watched this all from my desk, initially confused

*names are changed to protect confidentiality

by what I saw. Eventually the employee who initiated the game asked me to join (my door was wide open and I was clearly showing signs of interest). I participated in the game until someone dropped the ball and everyone started laughing hysterically. The ball was put away and everyone returned to their work without a sound. I remember smiling afterwards, feeling oddly refreshed. *What just happened?* I'll tell you. My colleagues had just engaged in an activity that broke up the monotony of the day and made them smile. The entire activity lasted about six minutes, hardly enough time to impede productivity. What it did do, though, was reenergize the group. It gave them a short break and made them feel human for a few minutes. No one stopped them, yelled at them or made them feel stupid about it. How amazing is that? I do understand that there is a time and place for everything, of course. I wouldn't encourage a game of catch at the office when visitors are in the building or you're in the middle of a state audit. However, supporting your employees as they find opportunities for fun (as they define it) throughout their work day can build trust, boost morale, and encourage a positive workplace culture. How are you creating or encouraging these moments with your employees?

*names are changed to protect confidentiality

## CHAPTER THREE:
# WORKING WITH "DIFFICULT" EMPLOYEES

Every manager, director, and CEO has, at one point or another, had to work with a difficult employee. The idea that all your staff will respect you and follow your directives with great pride every day is a lie. The idea that you will be loved and admired by all is a delusion. Leading other people is *hard* and one of the reasons for this is that you have to oversee the work of people with all kinds of personalities. Each and every one of your direct reports is a human being. That means that each person comes to work with his own set of vulnerabilities, insecurities, and personality flaws. They bring with them childhood and life experiences that can either set them

*names are changed to protect confidentiality

up to build healthy professional relationships or build relational walls created with blocks of resentment, fear, and anger.

Here are examples of life events that can profoundly impact an employee's ability to relate to their manger in manner that is professional, trusting, and collaborative:

- Childhood abuse (emotional, physical, or sexual)
- Childhood neglect
- Trauma (in any form)
- Illness
- Growing up in a high-crime neighborhood
- Unhealthy relationships with primary caregivers
- Drug abuse
- Domestic violence
- Previous negative experiences with an employer
- Organizational change without proper leadership
- Wrongful termination

In many of these cases, trust was broken. The employee learned (in childhood or later in life) to either keep their distance from people *or* attack them in some way in order to defend themselves and ensure their own survival. And here they are, in front

*names are changed to protect confidentiality

of you, giving you a hard time by not meeting deadlines, behaving unprofessionally, and making your job harder than it already is.

I get it. You might be wondering, "I don't care what they went through. Stop giving me a hard time. I'm not to blame for their shitty childhood or the horrible boss they had five years ago." No. It's not your fault and it certainly isn't fair that you have to deal with someone who has a nasty attitude or isn't doing their job. Let's stop for a moment, though. Let's think about this another way.

**Most difficult employees aren't jerks.**
**They are simply misunderstood.**

Before you tell me that your job is not to be your employee's therapist, hear me out. Yes, you are all there to do a job. No, it isn't your fault if your employee has emotional problems or a traumatic past. However, it is your responsibility to take these experiences into account and find a way to bring out the best in them. In some cases, you may do everything possible to build the relationship and improve performance only to find no improvement. That's fine. Before you get rid of the person, though, you must do your due diligence and try whatever you can to help makes things better for yourself and the employee.

Step one is to change your attitude. Notice I didn't say change the employee's attitude. *Your attitude.* In order to lead effectively, you must first identify (very clearly) what it is about this employee that you find to be difficult. Whatever the answer, make sure your language here is clear and specific. I don't want you telling

*names are changed to protect confidentiality

me that Sarah is difficult because she has an attitude problem or that Sanjay is difficult because he doesn't volunteer for extra projects. These definitions are broad and also dangerously subjective. I can't do anything with "has an attitude." If your description of your problem child doesn't include a list of measurable behaviors supported by specific examples, you're in trouble. Furthermore, this is an indication that the employee may not be the problem at all. It might be *you*. At this point, you want to ask yourself why this person is triggering you. Do they remind you of someone you don't like or someone who has hurt you in the past? Dig deep. Self-awareness is key here because if your feelings are personal, you cannot lead effectively.

Now, I might describe a truly difficult employee as someone who is late to work an average of four days a week, has received negative feedback from three clients in a year, and has demonstrated an unwillingness to attend all three recommended communication skills trainings. See the difference? Fact over perception. A (truly) difficult employee's behavior affects the team or company's ability to meet its targets, secure clients, and build a collaborative, trusting culture.

Once you've successfully described the employee's behaviors in measurable terms, you can continue to step two. In this next phase, you will hold a 1:1 meeting with the employee to level set. The goal here will be to get an understanding of how the employee defines success in their role. Simply ask, "Sarah, what does success look like for you here in the department?" Then, *let Sarah speak*. Really listen with an open mind and heart. Ask

*names are changed to protect confidentiality

Sarah whether, based on her definition, she has been successful lately. Again, let her talk. Ask open-ended questions. Describe to the employee what success in this role looks like for you and then list out the specific behaviors you've observed that go against that definition. Take some time to see if you can get to a definition of success that works for both of you. Take responsibility for your role as a leader by asking, "What specifically can I do to help you be successful?"

Hopefully, at this point, you will have some insight into the employee's experience along with a *shared definition of success*. This is a great starting point!

Assuming all is going well up to this point, step three is to take a step back and develop a different, more *individualized* approach with Sarah. Go back to the drawing board and get to know the employee all over again. Using her communication style and information collected during the 1:1 as the foundation, design a new strategy for engaging the employee. Check in often along the way to hold both of you accountable and show that the employee's success is a priority.

What if Sarah is not open to your question? What if she brushes it off, unwilling to engage with you? As I've said before, you are the leader, so it's up to you dig deeper. Be in the moment! Let Sarah know what you're seeing (maybe even feeling) in the moment. It sounds like this: "Sarah, I'm feeling that there's a wall between us right now. I'd like for you to be successful and happy here. However, I'm going to need your help to do that. Are you open to working with me to get you there?" Sarah's answer at this

*names are changed to protect confidentiality

point will tell you everything you need to know. If she continues to be closed off, behaves aggressively, or makes no attempt to improve her performance, you have to seriously consider whether termination is the best option.

*names are changed to protect confidentiality

# CHAPTER FOUR:
# TEAM MEETINGS

Staff meetings and individual check-ins are required for information sharing and team building. As a leader, it is your responsibility to meet with your people *in person* on a consistent basis, both as a group and individually, to assess needs, provide training, and receive feedback. This is true regardless of the industry you work in, whether it is the corporate sector, an educational setting, a non-profit organization, or the automobile industry. Many of you will say, "Monica I don't have the time in my day for this!" or "I have over 100 employees reporting to me; it's just not realistic." To me, those are excuses and a clear indication of managing instead of leading. How on earth can you build people up or ensure that they are performing at an optimal level when you don't meet with them regularly? How will you defend a lawsuit against a former employee if you don't have the documentation to show that you met regularly

*names are changed to protect confidentiality

to provide supervision and help them succeed in their role? The answer is that *you can't*.

> **To lead effectively, you must develop a system that works for you to meet with team members regularly.**

I don't care if you can only meet with them once every two months via skype or once a month for 30 thirty minutes. Just do it! Trust me, you won't regret it. The design and structure of your meeting is critical and should be planned out carefully in advance. The manner in which you start the meeting, the way in which information is relayed and prioritized, and the interactions you have with each employee must also be balanced. This means that there must be an equal focus on building relationships and achieving tasks during the meeting. You cannot hold a group of team members hostage for two hours as you spit out numbers, statistics, and a list of deadlines. Only managers do that. To achieve balance, you need to include several opportunities for team building in each meeting. This comes in the form of ice breakers, small physical activities, and opportunities for discussion. It also includes open-ended questions, such as "What are we doing well?" and "What can I do to support you better?" This focus on the relational *in addition to* the functional is the perfect combination for inspiring excellence in your team.

During your meetings, make sure that you, as the leader are the quietest person in the room. You want to say things, of course,

*names are changed to protect confidentiality

or else people might think you're not engaged. What I am suggesting is that you stop yourself from *running* the meeting. Avoid the impulse to bark orders at your team or spend the full hour telling them what to do.

## Meetings are transactional.

Remember we talked about trust earlier? Meetings are a great place to show your team that you trust them. Fall back and let them lead the meeting. I always tell my coaching clients, "Identify two-three measurable objectives for each meeting and then shut up." It is your job as the leader to lay the groundwork for the meeting and then allow your team to take the reins. If your team loses focus, bring them back. If your team is unable to identify solutions, ask open-ended questions that will inspire strategic thinking. By talking less and observing more, you will be able to look at things from a wider lens. You will be able to see things that you might not otherwise see if you were talking the whole time.

What should you be looking for? What should you be paying attention to? Well, *everything*. Observe how your employees talk to one another. Take notice of how ideas come together. How do team members interact with one another? Is one person taking over the meeting while others sit quietly or is everyone taking part in the discussion. Take a look at nonverbal communication. Team members may say they agree with an idea, but their body language or facial expressions may tell a different story.

*names are changed to protect confidentiality

Take all of this in and then draw some conclusions about any actions that might need to be taken. Do you need to schedule some 1:1s to address individual issues? Do your priorities need to change? Is your team lacking your support in some way? Are you losing someone in the group (emotionally)? By falling back, speaking less, and focusing on the bigger picture, you are better positioned to make decisions that are strategically aligned with the company's mission and financial objectives.

When you do speak, let it be for the purpose of clarifying, guiding, inspiring, or redirecting. Don't speak just to hear yourself talk. When asking questions or making comments, be sure to flex your style to fit the communication style of the person you're talking to. Be clear and concise when speaking to your direct employee. Be friendly and warm when speaking to your influence style employee. Slow down your speech and show appreciation when speaking to your steady style employee. With your conscientious style employee, speak to the facts and present information in a logical, well organized manner. When addressing a group with various communication styles, it's important to include a bit of each communication style in your presentation.

**Remember: leaders are flexible in thought and in approach.**

Your meeting should end on time (or as close to on time as possible). If you do need to go over the allotted time, let people know in advance if possible and explain why this is necessary. Do

*names are changed to protect confidentiality

not, I repeat, *do not* continue talking past the end time without acknowledging that you are about to go over time and providing some short (but meaningful explanation).

To ensure the best use of everyone's time, reserve at least five minutes at the end of the meeting to review the meeting objectives, any conclusions you've made, and next steps for each agenda item. Be sure that every person in the meeting is clear on the actions they need to take and the impact these actions will have on the business/team/unit.

How should people feel after leaving your meeting?

You want your people to leave each meeting feeling empowered and focused. A feeling of empowerment comes from feeling that your boss respects your time, your ideas, and your experience. Focus comes from being abundantly clear about what was discussed, what needs to be done next, and why it matters. When employees feel empowered and focused, they are more likely to carry out tasks in an efficient manner. They are more likely to execute with intention and strategy. They are also more likely to work as a team.

*names are changed to protect confidentiality

# CHAPTER FIVE:
# MEASURING SUCCESS

**Employees are much more likely to produce for the company if they feel respected, appreciated, and empowered.**

Effective leaders get results. Period. They know how to bring about the best in their people and they have the data to back it up. Think back to the best boss you've ever had. They probably inspired you to do great things. They supported you, coached you according to your strengths, and pushed you to go above what you thought was possible.

As a leader, your success is your employee's success. A leader will put an employee in a position to shine, so that they can achieve

*names are changed to protect confidentiality

their professional goals and ultimately, the company's mission. See what I did there? Notice that I mentioned the employee's goals first and *then* the company's mission. Successful leaders know that employees are much more likely to produce for the company if they feel respected, appreciated, and empowered.

Have you skipped this critical step in the process? Have you skipped over the employee's experience and jumped right to what they can do for your company? If so, it's time to take a step back. Invest time and resources to make sure that your team members feel good about their individual success *as well as* the company's success. As one of my coaching clients told me, "Once I feel that I'm valued and my individual happiness matters, I am all in. It's at that point that I feel motivated to do what's best for the company. I become all I can be for the company because I know that I matter to them."

Assuming that you've done everything I've outlined in the book so far and you've successfully engaged your employee, it's now time to look at how you can measure each person's success in order to sustain it.

## Defining Success

Success is a relative term. It can mean different things to different people. For some, success is tied to profit. For others, success is tied to client relationships, customer satisfaction, or overall productivity. A good leader understands that in order to ensure each employee's success, they must fully understand what success means

*names are changed to protect confidentiality

for each team member. You must also, of course, understand what success means (and looks like) for the company.

> **If you're not setting clear, measurable goals, how will you or your employee know if they are successful?**

Once you've established trust with the employee (as I've outlined in previous chapters), you can start setting goals. This process should be collaborative in nature and should incorporate the company's mission, the goals of the department, the employee's strengths and interests, and your needs.

I am a huge fan of using OKRs (objective and key results) as a measuring tool for success. If you don't know too much about OKRs, I suggest you start reading up on them now. The idea is pretty simple: set clear objectives and then develop a metric for how the employee will achieve those goals. These can't just be any objectives, though. They have to be the RIGHT objectives. Consider the following: Are you measuring what matters most to the company, the department, the team, and the employee? Are your objectives in line with what is valued by your customer, client, or audience?

Establish three-five objectives with each of your employees as early on in the relationship as possible. Designate times for reviewing progress toward goal attainment. Adjust goals as necessary. Create new goals/objectives as needed.

*names are changed to protect confidentiality

Here's what this might look like:

............................................................

**OBJECTIVE** *(goal)*

Improve customer service for first quarter

............................................................

**KEY RESULTS**

*(how you will measure progress towards that goal)*

1. Improve customer satisfaction survey scores by at least 20 percent.

2. Complete professional development training on active listening.

3. Meet with executive coach 1x a week to improve communication skills training.

............................................................

Whether you use this framework or something similar to it, the point is to *track* your employees' success, so that both you and your team member can stay focused and productive. Without a tracking system, you run the risk of leading a team that has no direction, no accountability, and no real urgency for getting things done.

*names are changed to protect confidentiality

**CHAPTER SIX:**

# HOW TO KEEP YOURSELF MOTIVATED

Effective leaders work hard, really hard. They dedicate a great deal of time and energy to building their brand, coaching their employees, and achieving (measurable) results for their company. You know by now that this is no easy feat.

Before I send you off into the real world to build powerful teams and inspire greatness in others, we need to talk about how to care for your most important team member – you. Sounds weird, doesn't it? We've spent the majority of this book talking about how to help others achieve greatness through your leadership. Well, the truth is that eventually, everyone has to go home or log off. Eventually, you need to give yourself some attention, so that you

*names are changed to protect confidentiality

have enough fuel to do it all over again the next day. As a leader, you will have to manage crises, put in long hours, deal with difficult employees/clients, and push yourself to levels you've never thought possible. You may have secretly shed a few tears after a challenging day or frustrating encounter with an employee or partner.

Through all the hard work, all the sacrifices, and all the sleepless nights, leaders must find a way to keep themselves going for the sake of the team. You are their fearless warrior – the one they turn to for answers, encouragement, and guidance. *They need you.* But… who takes care of *you*? How will you make sure that *you* are operating from a place of strength? How will you stay motivated during those times when leadership itself feels exhausting?

Some leaders are fortunate enough to have a strong network they can turn to for support, guidance, and inspiration. Others can rely only on themselves for motivation. At the end of the day, regardless of your situation, you are the only person who can keep yourself going. *You* are the only person who is responsible for taking care of yourself.

## How can leaders care for themselves and stay motivated?

First things first, let's take a moment to acknowledge that you are human. You might be a super powerful leader with amazing abilities and talents but you're still human. Being human means that you (at times) will feel fear, anger, frustration and a host of other emotions. I remember the first time I fired someone. I was

*names are changed to protect confidentiality

beyond nervous. My stomach hurt, my chest was pounding, and I wanted to run away as fast as I could. I felt scared and I felt guilty. I knew I was doing the right thing, but nevertheless I felt extreme anxiety. I vividly remember hearing my voice crack as I dismissed my employee from her position. Years later, I came to see that what I experienced was normal. I was having a natural, human response to an uncomfortable situation. Firing someone for the first time was not easy but I learned over the years to cut myself some slack and allowed myself to feel whatever emotions came up for me.

To remain successful, you need to care for yourself and invest in your own well-being. You spend your time developing your team, nurturing their ideas, and supporting their growth but you put yourself *last*?

No, no, no. This is no different than being a parent. As caregivers, we give and give and give. At some point, however, we need to also prioritize our own needs, desires, and goals. That way, we can give our children the best of what we have to give. As a leader, you must do the same thing.

## To give the best of yourself, you must care for yourself *first*.

Most leaders are not surrounded by a team of people rooting for them or a group of experts guiding their next move. Unless you've hired a coach or are blessed to have a mentor, chances are that you're doing this all alone.

*names are changed to protect confidentiality

…And I mean *alone*. It's true what they say. It *is* lonely at the top. The higher you go up the ladder, the more alone you will probably feel. Being the boss comes with natural consequences, including the reality of having to be your own motivator.

You might think, "Well, my employees support me. They are like my friends." *Wrong*. Your employees are your employees. You are in a position of power over them, so behaving as though you're on an equal plane is a huge mistake. You might think, "Well, I have my own boss to lean on." Wonderful! Having a supportive boss helps a lot but they have their own problems and are not always going to be around.

Ultimately, it's going to be up to *you* to keeps yourself going, so listen up. The first thing I want you to do is engage in regular self-care. That's right. I want you to treat yourself as an important part of the team. That means getting good rest (staying up working until 3 a.m. every night does not make you a hero). It means eating right and getting regular exercise. It means treating yourself well, so that you have enough energy (mental and physical) left over for your team.

Here are some more ways to take care of yourself:

- Prepare for your week on Sundays
- Practice meditation
- Keep up with your physical appearance

*names are changed to protect confidentiality

- Establish boundaries (you don't always have to answer the phone or send an email immediately)
- Read for pleasure
- Find a new hobby
- Take time for your family

Even with proper self-care, it can be challenging to keep yourself motivated. Here are some tips for staying on track:

- Remember your "why" (why did you get into this work? Why is it important to you? How does it impact people's lives?)
- Build your confidence. In order to achieve greatness, you must remember how amazing you are. Keep telling yourself, "I can do this." Control your thoughts because they will determine your attitude when things go wrong and your behavior when it's time to take action.
- Surround yourself with greatness. The people around us can either motivate us or drain us! Be sure to nurture relationships that can help you when things get tough. Look for people that listen without judgment, give honest feedback, and are doing amazing things themselves. #TeamExcellence

*names are changed to protect confidentiality

## Final Thoughts

Leadership is a privilege. It's an opportunity to help people reach their full potential, so that a common goal can be achieved. In order to be successful, leaders must be intentional, strategic, and collaborative. They must understand the incredible power that comes with managing others and do what it takes to nurture those relationships.

Leaders achieve greatness by investing in themselves first and then transferring that energy over to their biggest investors – their employees. They lead with confidence but also a great deal of humility, understanding that trust is the foundation on which great teams are built.

I thank you for reading this book and taking the time to learn about yourself as a leader. Your willingness to tackle some of the subjects presented tells me that you take your role seriously. Remember to give the best of yourself each and every day, so that you can ask others to do the same for you and your company.

Good is not good enough. Be excellent!

Sincerely,

Monica Guzman

Executive Coach | Motivational Speaker

*names are changed to protect confidentiality